Your Body and You

BODY PRIVACY

By Anita Ganeri

Illustrated by Vera Popova

PowerKiDS press

Published in 2025 by The Rosen Publishing Group, Inc.
2544 Clinton Street, Buffalo, NY 14224

Credits

Series editor: Julia Bird
Illustrator: Vera Popova
Packaged by: Collaborate

Cataloging-in-Publication Data

Names: Ganeri, Anita, 1961-, author. | Popova, Vera, illustrator.
Title: Body privacy / by Anita Ganeri, illustrated by Vera Popova.
Description: Buffalo, NY : Powerkids Press, 2025. | Series: Your body and you | Includes glossary and index.
Identifiers: ISBN 9781499445466 (pbk.) | ISBN 9781499445473 (library bound) | ISBN 9781499445480 (ebook)
Subjects: LCSH: Interpersonal relations in children--Juvenile literature. | Personal space--Juvenile literature. | Privacy--Juvenile literature. | Human body--Juvenile literature. | Boundaries (Psychology)--Juvenile literature.
Classification: LCC BF723.I646 G326 2025 | DDC 155.4'18 --dc23

Manufactured in the United States of America
CPSIA Compliance Information: Batch #CSPK25. For further information contact Rosen Publishing at 1-800-237-9932.

CONTENTS

IT'S MY BODY!

Your body is amazing.

Just think of all the things your body can do!

It can move around.

It helps you think, talk, laugh and sing.

It grows bigger and stronger.

It mends itself if you get hurt.

It's important to look after your amazing body, and keep it working well. You can do this by eating healthy food, drinking lots of water, and staying fit.

Make sure you get enough sleep, too. Your hardworking body needs plenty of rest.

You also need to keep your body safe. This means things like wearing a seat belt in the car, and looking both ways (and then looking again!) before you cross the road. It also means remembering your body belongs to you. You choose what you want to do with it. You decide who can touch you.

DIFFERENT TOUCHES

There are different kinds of touch - good and bad.

Good touches make you feel safe.
They feel caring and comforting.

They are touches like ...

... a hug from your dad
when you fall off your bike.

... a bedtime kiss
from your mom.

... your grandpa
holding your hand
to cross the road.

Bad touches make you feel unsafe. They can hurt you or make you feel scared. They are touches like...

... someone hitting or pinching you.

... someone pulling your hair.

... someone touching you in a private place.

... ANY touches that you don't like and want to stop.

This book will tell you more about the different kinds of touches, and what you should do to keep your body safe.

FEELING GOOD

People may touch you for different reasons.

You might get lifted up and hugged by your favorite aunt or uncle when they come to visit.

Your mom or dad might give you a hug after you've had a bad day at school.

You might have a group hug with your teammates when you score the winning goal.

Good touches can make you feel happy and safe. But sometimes, you might not want to be hugged or kissed. You might not feel like it. You might feel shy or embarrassed. It's okay to say you don't want to, even if it's a person you know and love. Ask them to blow you a kiss, give you a high five or shake your hand instead.

DON'T TOUCH!

Some touches are not okay. They can hurt you or make you feel uncomfortable.

Someone might push you over on the playground on purpose. Someone might kick or pinch you.

Remember, it's your body and you get to choose what happens to it. If you can, tell the person to stop what they are doing. If they don't stop, tell a teacher or another adult you can trust.

What if a friend or sibling starts tickling you, and you don't like it? They don't mean to hurt you, and think you're both having fun.

It's still okay to tell them you don't like it. You can still ask them to stop.

PRIVATE PARTS

Some parts of your body are private.

These are the parts you cover with your underwear or swimsuit. They are the parts you don't usually show to other people. They are private to you.

Like the rest of your body, your private parts are important. It's very normal to want to know about them and how they work. But remember that they are private. You shouldn't touch them or look at them when you're with other people.

Naming private parts

You might know your private parts by different names or even nicknames, but the correct names for a boy's private parts are penis and testicles, while a girl has a vagina.

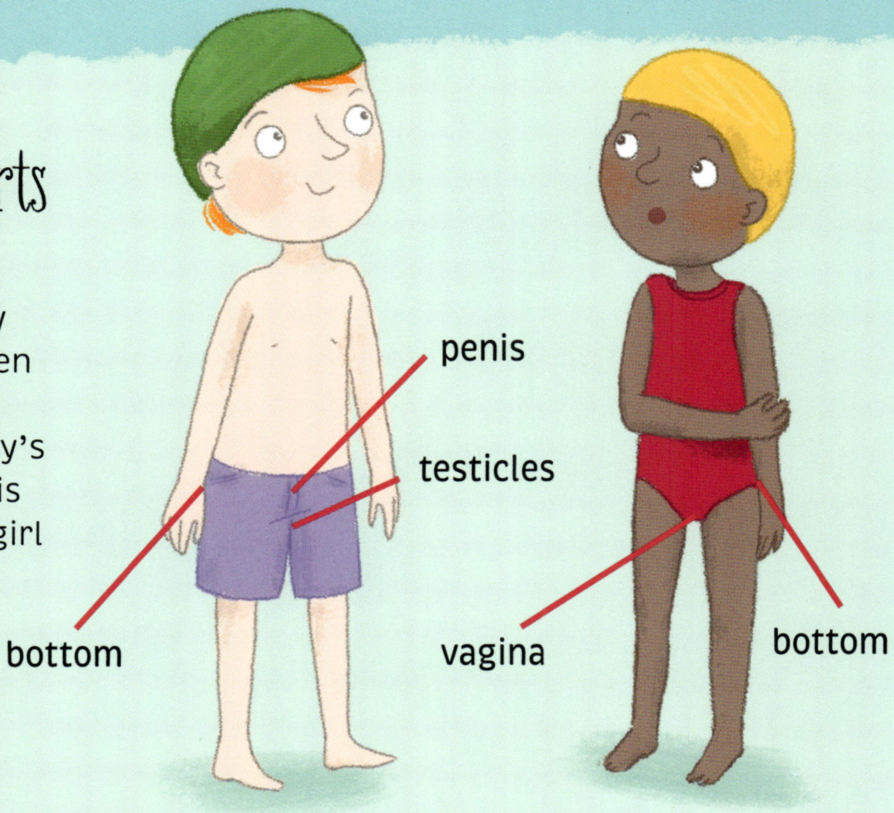

TAKING CARE

Sometimes, your parents, caregivers or a doctor may need to see your private parts.

They may need to touch them to check you are well. They will explain what they're doing and ask you if that's okay. Your parent or caregiver will stay with you while the doctor examines you. If you're not comfortable with anything, you must say so.

The doctor is trying to help you. He or she wants to make sure you're healthy and well. But it is never okay for anyone to see or touch your private parts unless they are helping you. It doesn't matter if you know the person or not. It doesn't matter if they are male or female. It doesn't matter if they are an adult or a child.

KEEPING SECRETS

Are you good at keeping secrets?

Some secrets can be fun, like your friend's surprise birthday party, or the special meal you are planning for your mom.

But not all secrets are like that. Some secrets can be upsetting, or make you feel scared. What if someone hurts you, or touches your private parts? Then they might ask you to keep this a secret, or threaten to hurt you if you tell. This is never okay.

These are bad secrets. You don't need to keep secrets like these. It's important to tell someone you can trust, even if you've promised not to say anything. You never have to keep a secret that makes you feel unhappy or uncomfortable.

TELLING SOMEONE

If someone touches you and you don't want them to, say no. Say it, or shout it as loudly as you can. Keep on saying or shouting it. Then run or get away from the person as quickly as possible.

Don't keep what's happened to yourself. It is really important to tell someone. Talk to your mom, dad, or another trusted adult, like your teacher or the school nurse.

If you're worried about what to say, why not try:

I want to tell you something, but it's meant to be secret.

Something bad has happened, and I don't know what to do.

I want to tell you something, but I'm scared you'll be mad.

Telling someone will make you feel better. But if you find it too hard to talk to someone, you can draw a picture of what happened, or write it down instead.

FEELING HURT

Being hurt or touched in a bad way can make you feel sad and scared. You might feel embarrassed. You might feel ashamed.

You might think it's better to keep what's happened to yourself. You don't want to tell anyone in case you get into trouble. Worse still, you're worried that the person won't believe you.

DID YOU KNOW?

Your feelings can be hurt in other ways, too. If someone calls you names, shouts at you, or makes you feel bad, tell your trusted adult.

All of these feelings are real and important. They can make you feel very unhappy and alone. But remember, you are not to blame. There is no need to feel it's your fault.

You might feel like running away. You might not want to go to school. You might just want to hide in your room. But these won't make your feelings go away. The best way to feel safe again is to tell someone you trust. It's never too late.

SAFE ONLINE

The Internet is a great place to learn, have fun, and keep in touch. But, just as in the real world, it's important to keep yourself safe online.

Millions of people use the Internet, all over the world. Some of them are friends. But most of them are strangers. Sometimes, strangers might trick you into becoming their friend.

They may trick you into telling them private things about yourself. They might try to make you look at websites that aren't suitable for children. They may even try to meet you in real life. NEVER arrange to meet anyone you meet online in real life. They could turn out to be someone who wants to do you harm.

Always be careful about what you click on when you're online. Not everything you see or read on the Internet is suitable for children. There are good and bad websites, and good and bad apps. Some report news that is deliberately wrong. This might be to scare you, or to get money from you.

DID YOU KNOW?

Parents or caregivers can set up parental controls on tablets, phones, and other devices you use. This helps make sure you only see things that are safe for you.

CYBERBULLYING

Bullying can happen in lots of places - at school, at home, or online. When bullying happens online, it is called cyberbullying.

Cyberbullying is when someone posts or likes nasty photos or comments about you online. The bully could be someone you know, or a stranger you've never met. It's horrible and upsetting. It's also against the law.

IMPORTANT!

If this happens to you, tell a trusted adult immediately. Don't share or reply to the bully's posts. Show them to your trusted adult. They will know what to do.

Here are some more top tips for staying safe online:

- Keep your address, school, and phone number private.
- Only chat to real-life friends and family, not to strangers.
- Never tell anyone your password, even your best friend.

- Don't say anything nasty about anyone, even if it's a joke.
- If you're upset by anything you see online, tell your trusted adult.
- Only post pictures you would be happy for your parents or teachers to see.

SMARTPHONE SAFETY

You might have a smartphone of your own, or you might just borrow your mom's or dad's sometimes.

You can use a smartphone for lots of things, so you need to keep it, and you, safe. Even if you're careful, things can still go wrong.

You might see or share something you shouldn't.

You might lose or break the phone.

Don't worry, there are lots of things that can help. Many are the same as for staying safe online.

If you take a phone out with you, keep it in a safe place where it's out of sight. Try not to let anyone else use it if possible.

A phone also works as a camera. You can snap pictures on it all day long. But be careful not to share anything you wouldn't want your parents or teachers to see.

Be careful who you talk to. If you get a call from a stranger, or a number you don't know, end the call. Tell your trusted adult.

If you have your own phone, add a parent's or caregiver's phone number to the contacts. If something happens to you, someone can get in touch with them.

YOU'RE IN CONTROL

Your body is yours, and belongs to you. You're in control, and get to choose what happens to it.

No one else has the right to touch you, or make you feel uncomfortable, whether online or in real life. It doesn't matter who they are. If you ask them to stop, they should stop. Make sure you tell a trusted adult about anything that makes you feel unhappy or worried.

Listen to your body, and take care of how you're feeling - bad or good. Bad things can sometimes happen. But remember, a big hug from someone you love and trust can be the best feeling in the world!

GLOSSARY

Caregiver
Someone who looks after another person.

Deliberately
Done on purpose.

Device
Electronic equipment, such as a smartphone or tablet.

Embarrassed
Feeling awkward or uncomfortable.

Examine
To look at carefully.

Online
Connected to the Internet.

Password
Secret word or phrase used on a computer.

Private
Belonging to a person and not to others.

Private parts
Parts of your body that are covered by a swimsuit.

Sibling
Brother or sister.

Trust
To rely on someone to help you.

Trusted adult
A grown-up whom you trust and can talk to about anything. It could be a relative, close family friend, or teacher.

FIND OUT MORE

Websites

https://stopitnow.org/?gclid=CjwKCAiAibeuBhAAEiwAiXBoJGxmH9GGZAevpjI-LFFxmF5ANFun NQXa7csCI9beEhaMRqhuGXIrrxoCoeEQAvD_BwE

Stop It Now! is an organization that mobilizes families and communities to prevent the abuse of children.

https://www.zeroabuseproject.org/victim-assistance/jwrc/keep-kids-safe/

This website features a list of concepts to help keep children and teens safe from harm.

www.bbc.co.uk/bitesize/clips/z3xb9qt

Facts, figures and video clips about your amazing body, and how it works.

Books

My Life: Being Safe
Sarah Ridley, PowerKids Press 2023

Under Our Clothes: Our First Talk About Our Bodies

Jillian Roberts, Orca Book Publishers 2020

It's My Body: A Book About Body Privacy for Young Children

Louise Spilsbury, Franklin Watts 2020

INDEX